The Symbols & Traditions of Yule

This book

belongs to:

Evergreen trees represent being resilient through the long winter months. They were often decorated with food and berries for the forest spirits and bells for them to ring as a thank you for the food and warmth.

Traditionally, **ornaments** were made of berries and other treats and cakes and often strung together to make a garland. Today we use colorful ornaments of all different shapes and colors.

The star represents the elements and is a reminder of the importance of them in all parts of our life.

Earth, Air, Fire, Water, and Spirit

Elves help protect our house and often leave little gifts during Yule, but be careful... If we aren't nice to them or each other, they can be naughty and leave messes for us to clean up.

Candles symbolize the warmth of the Sun and the Sun's light returning to the Earth.

Gingerbread became apart of Yule and the Winter Solstice because ginger was such a rare spice that it was only used around this time of year.

Reindeer are a symbol of creativity and safe travels through the harsh winter and have come to be represented by pulling Santa's sleigh.

Santa Claus has many names, depending on where you live. He inspires us to give without measure and to help those in need without seeking treasure.

Wassail is a traditional drink for Yule that is often made of apple cider with yummy spices like cinnamon and star anise.

Holly is often used to decorate the outside of the home for protection with their red berries and pointed leaves, it also represents The Holly King.

The **wreath** represents the wheel of life and that the cycles are never ending. We decorate them with holly, ivy, pine cones, berries and bows.

Bells were often rung to chase away any bad spirits and to convince the sun to return. They were also hung in the tree for the spirits or elves to ring.

We give **presents** to celebrate the birth of the sun and the light returning, but also to celebrate each other and show our appreciation.

The **Yule log** was kept burning throughout the celebration of yule for twelve days and nights.

Mistletoe is all about love and romance, believed to come from ancient Roman celebrations, but the Celts used it for its healing properties... so if you're under the mistletoe, pucker up!

Stockings represent shoes that children left out with hay for the reindeer and they hoped Santa would fill them with gifts as a thank you.

Winter Activities

Picking out a tree, whether its from a tree lot, a box or the forest. This is a tradition that should stick around!

Decorating the tree to get ready to celebrate the holiday

Decking the halls with evergreens, stockings bows and holly to bring in the spirit of the season.

Making our wish list for Santa and our parents.

Making cookies and treats for our family and friends.

Wrapping presents to
give to others

Ice Skating is a super fun way to celebrate the outdoors and the colder months.

Enjoying a cup of **hot chocolate** to warm up after ice skating

Building a
snowman and having
snowball fights!

Igloo Snow forts are so much fun to build if you have a good amount of snow where you live.

Family dinner was common in ancient times and is still the most common activity during Yule to date.

Decorating
Gingerbread houses is a
fun way to spend a winter
day inside and they taste
delicious too!

Sledding with family and friends is so much fun!

No matter how you choose to celebrate this magical time of year, Give when you can and spread some holiday cheer!

Happy Yule!

Made in the USA
Monee, IL
18 December 2022

22557316R00040

The Humble Sage

ISBN 9798766365570

9 798766 365570